T0319007

THE STUDY OF
AMERICAN HISTORY

THE STUDY
OF
AMERICAN HISTORY

BY

VISCOUNT BRYCE, O.M.

BEING THE INAUGURAL LECTURE OF THE
SIR GEORGE WATSON CHAIR OF AMERICAN
HISTORY, LITERATURE AND INSTITUTIONS

WITH AN APPENDIX RELATING TO
THE FOUNDATION

CAMBRIDGE
AT THE UNIVERSITY PRESS
1921

CAMBRIDGE
UNIVERSITY PRESS

University Printing House, Cambridge CB2 8BS, United Kingdom

Published in the United States of America by Cambridge University Press, New York

Cambridge University Press is part of the University of Cambridge.

It furthers the University's mission by disseminating knowledge in the pursuit of
education, learning and research at the highest international levels of excellence.

www.cambridge.org
Information on this title: www.cambridge.org/9781107639515

© Cambridge University Press 1921

This publication is in copyright. Subject to statutory exception
and to the provisions of relevant collective licensing agreements,
no reproduction of any part may take place without the written
permission of Cambridge University Press.

First published 1921
First paperback edition 2014

A catalogue record for this publication is available from the British Library

ISBN 978-1-107-63951-5 Paperback

Cambridge University Press has no responsibility for the persistence or accuracy of
URLs for external or third-party internet websites referred to in this publication,
and does not guarantee that any content on such websites is, or will remain, accurate
or appropriate.

PREFATORY NOTE

BY THE SECRETARY
OF THE ANGLO-AMERICAN SOCIETY

LORD BRYCE'S INAUGURAL LECTURE
under the Sir George Watson Foundation,
which is here presented to the public, was delivered
at the Mansion House, London, on Monday, June
27th, 1921, before a large and representative assem-
bly, including many American visitors. The Rt Hon.
Arthur J. Balfour, M.P., presided.

Mr H. S. Perris, the secretary of the Anglo-
American Society, read a letter from the Prince of
Wales's private secretary regretting that owing to
the pressure of public engagements the Prince was
unable to be present, "especially as this is a function
which it would have given him special pleasure to
attend, not only in view of the objects for which the
Anglo-American Society exists, but as a further
mark of his appreciation of Sir George Watson's
generosity."

Mr Balfour, who had to leave the Mansion House
before Lord Bryce had concluded his address in
order to attend the meeting of the Imperial Confer-
ence, said there could not be a more fitting opening
of what he hoped was going to be a fruitful course of
lectures delivered in this country by authorities upon

Anglo-American history than a lecture by Lord
Bryce himself. He had every qualification for the
task which he had so kindly undertaken. He had
made his name as an historian of European repute
much more than a generation ago, and that early
reputation of his had been sustained and increased
by all his subsequent work. He was not only a
trained historian and a universal traveller, but he
was also a special authority upon American subjects.
He approached questions dealing with America with
the special advantage that he knew the subject not
merely from books, not merely from the sources which
historians ordinarily drew upon in order to complete
their picture of the past; he had in addition to that
qualification, which he possessed in the fullest
measure, the practical experience which residence in
the United States had given him; a residence most
important from the immediate diplomatic point of
view, for he had to deal over and over again with
questions profoundly interesting to both the great
English-speaking peoples. In addition to that, he
made himself acquainted with, and, I think I may
say in the presence of American friends, beloved, by
every section of public opinion in America, irrespec-
tive of party, profession, tastes and all the other
varieties of interest which divide mankind. That is
a unique qualification. There is no man living who
possessed it in anything like the same measure as

Lord Bryce. Happy indeed were we to have secured his services on the present occasion.

Mr Balfour continued: I need not say anything more except that to promote the mutual comprehension of these two great Peoples seems to me the worthiest object which any man can propose to himself at the present time. I do not believe that there is any cause which involves greater consequences for the future of civilization. I do not believe that there is any end for which it is more worth while striving and struggling, and I rejoice to-day that this view is not only held by students and statesmen like Lord Bryce, but has appealed to men who, like my friend Sir George Watson, have the imaginative insight to see how wealth can best be used, and who now, not for the first time in his beneficent career, has expended great sums of money in a cause which I am quite confident will repay all the expectations which he has formed of it.

At the conclusion of Lord Bryce's lecture a vote of thanks to the Lord Mayor, to Mr Balfour, and to the Lecturer, was moved by Alderman Sir Charles Wakefield, Bart., Hon. Treasurer of the Anglo-American Society and of the Sulgrave Institution.

This was seconded by Dr Nicholas Murray Butler, President of Columbia University, New York, who said: "It is a privilege to be permitted on behalf of my countrymen, so many of whom are here present this afternoon, to second the vote of thanks to the Lord Mayor, to Mr Balfour, and to Lord Bryce, and I hope I may be permitted to add, to Sir George Watson, whose foresight and generosity have started a movement which one may confidently say is bound to have the largest and the happiest results. It would be unbecoming in me at this hour to detain you with any comments of my own, but perhaps I may say that the spirit in which Lord Bryce has approached his great subject this afternoon offers an introduction to the study of American history that is exceptionally inviting and exceptionally profitable. He has not chosen to dwell upon names or dates or purely political happenings and circumstances, but has rather sought for mention and emphasis those great underlying principles of social construction and of social and political interpretation which it has been, after all, the glory of the English-speaking peoples for a thousand years in so many ways to illustrate and to carry forward. I sincerely hope that this vote of thanks, which I am sure will be unanimously passed, will be the first of many witnesses of appreciation of successive lectures upon this foundation and of the generosity of him who has made it possible."

After some words in support of the Resolution by the Marquess of Aberdeen, the Resolution was put to the meeting and carried with acclamation.

CONTENTS

PAGE

PREFATORY NOTE v
BY THE SECRETARY OF THE ANGLO-AMERICAN
SOCIETY

THE STUDY OF AMERICAN HISTORY . 1
BY THE RT HON. VISCOUNT BRYCE, O.M.

APPENDIX 45
RELATING TO THE FOUNDATION AND PURPOSES
OF THE SIR GEORGE WATSON CHAIR OF AMERI-
CAN HISTORY, LITERATURE, AND INSTITUTIONS,
TOGETHER WITH A REPRINT OF THE ORIGINAL
CORRESPONDENCE RELATING THERETO

INDEX 59

PLATE

PORTRAIT OF SIR GEORGE WATSON . . TO FACE 45

THE STUDY OF
AMERICAN HISTORY

By the Rt Hon. Viscount Bryce, O.M.

MY first duty is, if I may venture to make myself the spokesman of British students of history, to express their thanks to the munificent founder of this professorial chair, whose enlightened vision has discerned what was lacking in the provision made for the study of American history in England, and who has by this foundation gone far to remedy that defect. I do not say that we in England have studied ancient history, or mediaeval history, or modern European history too much, but we have studied American history too little. How great is the gain to be expected from its study I shall presently try to indicate. For the moment let me be content to convey to the founder our sense of the great service his far-sighted generosity has rendered, and to express the confident hope that it will begin to bear abundant fruit.

What does American history mean? To ask this question is to ask: When does American history begin? To that question different answers may be given. Some will say it begins with the tribes who inhabited the North American continent from the era of immemorial darkness, before they came into contact with any white men, even with the Icelanders who sailed from Greenland in the ship of Leif the son of Eric. The only data we possess for the study of those prehistoric days are to be found in a study of the relations between the languages of the different aboriginal tribes, and in the scanty relics which have been preserved in their burial places, and especially in the great mounds they erected in the wide spreading plains of the Upper Mississippi.

Others will fix the beginning of American history in the earliest age of European colonization, that is to say, at the date of the enterprise attempted under Raleigh's auspices at Roanoke in 1585, or at the making of effective settlements at James Town in Virginia in 1607, and on the coast of Massachusetts by the Pilgrims in 1620. Many, however,—and I suspect they would include more than might be expected of the less educated citizens of the United States—would, if the question were suddenly put to them, reply that their history began with the Declaration of Independence in 1776, when the peoples of the Colonies disclaimed the authority of the British Crown, and started on their career as a group of associated Sovereign States.

All these answers err by thinking of the Country rather than of the People who inhabit the country. The history of the Land belongs to geology. The history of the aborigines, such as it is, belongs to the sciences of ethnology, philology, and folklore, and it is a history which has already come to its end. It was my good fortune to see the last two leading figures among the Indian tribes, one of them Sitting Bull, chief of the Sioux, in 1883, at the city of Bismarck, in Dakota; the other, Geronimo, chief of the Apaches of Arizona, at Fort Sell in Oklahoma in 1907. There are now probably not more than a few thousands of aboriginal Indians of pure stock still surviving, and their descendants will soon be lost, absorbed into the growing white population of the West. The Englishmen who landed in Virginia in 1607, and on the bleaker shores of Massachusetts thirteen years later, did not begin a new history, but continued a history which had begun many centuries before. When did that old history begin? We all remember the phrase with which Montesquieu surprised his contemporaries when he was describing to them the original lines of the English Constitution. "Ce beau systeme a été trouvé dans les bois." The history of those who settled North America began in the forests and on the shores of Holstein and East Frisia far back in days of which we have no native record save in mythology and poetry, in the worship of Woden and Thunor (Thunder) and Freya, and in the ancient lay of Beowulf. A branch of this Teutonic stock conquered Eastern, Southern and Central Britain, and ultimately, intermingled with the Celtic population which they found there, grew to be the English nation, which, by the beginning of the seventeenth century, was already, for those days, a large nation, possibly of four millions, as large as the Scottish people or the Swiss people are to-day, and smaller than the Bulgarians or the Portuguese. It was from a tiny body of settlers belonging to that English nation, reinforced by later English immigrants, and with the addition of some Hollanders, Swedes and Germans, that the American nation sprang.

Having already observed that the history of a nation is the history of the men who compose the nation, and not of their dwelling-place, and that it is, therefore, a record of what the men were and of what they did, let us consider what this includes. It includes, primarily, their character; that is to say, the distinctive quality of their habits of feeling, thinking and acting, and secondarily, the institutions, social and political, in which those habits found expression. Institutions, when solidified by long practice, come to be, because respected and valued, a permanent factor in moulding and developing character itself. In its earliest form the American stock was the small branch of a large race dwelling in the North Temperate zone, possessing already, in its old home on the European continent, certain distinctive gifts and qualities unlike those of the neighbouring racial stocks, Celtic,

Slavonic and Italic, and having also institutions, though still in a rudimentary stage. Julius Caesar and Tacitus tell us that there were in the Germanic tribes kings honoured for their lineage, war-leaders chosen for their bravery, and popular assemblies, in which the more important decisions were taken. We cannot talk of a Germanic Nation, but of tribes, branches of a widespread race, among them Angles, Jutes and Saxons, tribes often at war one with another, and as yet without a collective national consciousness. When some of these tribes settled in Britain, raiding north-ward and westward from the spots where their war bands landed, they were still no more than the raw material of a nation, but they grew in the course of centuries to be a national state, and by the four-teenth century they had acquired a definite type of character, which was finding its expression in litera-ture, and they had also created an elaborate system of institutions, including a legislature, partly repre-sentative, courts administering justice throughout the country, an executive government, co-operating with, yet sometimes in conflict with, the elected representatives of the people. Foreign observers in the fifteenth century, such as Froissart and Aeneas Sylvius Piccolomini (afterwards Pope Pius II) and Philip of Comines already talk of the English as a people quite unlike the peoples of the continent.

This may be called the second stage in the growth

of the American nation. The third stage begins when an extremely small branch is transplanted to a new continent. The first migration was from a continent to an island, the second was from an island to an immense continent. In that continent these transplanted Englishmen do not cease to be English, but they presently, though very slowly, develop into a different kind of English, under the new influences which began from the first to work upon them. Much later, when they were politically separated from the British Crown, a new name was needed to distinguish them from the English who had remained behind in the old Mother Land, and so the term "American," theretofore employed to denote the aboriginal Red Men, came to be applied to the English of America as being now an independent nation. The use of the word made a great difference, for words have a curious power of implicit suggestion, a power inevitable, but often misleading. In this case the name did mislead, and has gone on misleading. It made the less instructed part of the American nation forget the greatness of their spiritual heritage, and think of themselves as a new nation, when they were really part of an old nation to which their forefathers had belonged in those very days when it was reaching the highest level it has ever yet attained in poetry and thought. The age which sent Englishmen to settle in Virginia and Massachusetts was the age of Shakespeare and Spenser and Milton, of Bacon and Newton and Harvey, of Cromwell and Hampden and Jeremy Taylor and John Bunyan, glories of the English stock whom Americans have just as good a right to claim as has England herself. Thus the intellectual, moral and religious history of England for thirteen centuries, from the landing of the Jutish keels at Ebbsfleet in Kent in the middle of the fifth century A.D., is a part of American history. Whoever forgets this truth will fail to understand that history as a whole, in its most essential features.

We may now pass to that third stage in which American history begins to be the history of America only, i.e. of that branch of the English stock which came under a new set of influences peculiar to the new land, and was at the same time removed from some of the influences which were thereafter to affect the development of that then larger branch which, remaining in Britain, was in close contact with the European continent. But we must remember that the connecting influences of literature were still operative, because the language was the same, and all that was thought and written on either side of the Atlantic told upon men's minds on the other side. Bearing this in mind, let us consider what were the influences, peculiar to the new continent, which have slowly transformed the children of the English settlers of the seventeenth century into the Americans of the twentieth.

First, a word or two upon Climate. The land in which the immigrants settled lay further south than England, yet even in the northern part of it the winters were colder, though the summers were hotter, than in the same latitude in Europe. Climate is not to be measured by latitude, and in the northern part of the United States other factors, such as winds and ocean currents, have so moderated the summer heats as to enable the old Teutonic stock to remain fully as strong and physically vigorous as it was when it left its European home. Some observers think that the race has become more nervously excitable, and so more susceptible to new ideas and sudden accesses of emotion. Without venturing to controvert this view, I incline to believe that climate has done less to modify national character than is generally supposed, so far as the cooler parts of North America are concerned. When, however, we regard those parts which lie south of latitude $35°$ N. the case is different. Here, except in the hill-country, outdoor labour is, not indeed impossible, but unwelcome to a northern race. The settlers thought that in the regions south of the Potomac and the Ohio they must procure some other kind of labour than their own to cultivate the land, so the example which had been set by the Spaniards in the Antilles was unfortunately followed. Negroes were brought from Africa to work as slaves, and thus in the southern colonies there grew up a social system quite different from that of the northern regions, in which the white owner had been tilling his own farm. When, owing to the invention of labour-saving machinery, the cultivation of cotton became so huge and highly profitable an industry, that immense quantities of that fibre were thenceforth sent to the markets of Europe, the welfare of the inhabitants of the South was deemed to be bound up with the maintenance of slavery. Estates were large, a planting oligarchy grew up and controlled politics, the humbler part of the white population sank into a condition far below that of the northern whites. Whether the character of the Southern people has been permanently affected may be doubted, for the old planting aristocracy has now almost disappeared, while the poorer element among the whites has risen. But it must be confessed that the respect felt for justice, law and order was more or less temporarily impaired, and the habit of lynching has not yet vanished. As you all know, the presence of a negro population exceeding ten millions remains a source of trouble and disquiet.

Another new factor that told upon the character of the race in its new home, was the absence in the earlier days of some of the external appliances of civilization, and the consequent need imposed upon the settler of self-help and individual exertion. It was only at intervals that attacks by the Indian aborigines were to be feared, but Nature has had always to be resisted and overcome, and the effort to subdue her evoked energy and became a spur to invention. To this let us add that in the northern states the settlers found themselves relieved from the pressure of a territorial aristocracy such as had maintained social inequalities in England. The American cultivator, especially in the north, owned his land, and until the middle of the nineteenth century no great fortunes were amassed in trade or manufacturing industry. Conditions so favourable to social equality had existed nowhere in Europe except in rural Switzerland and in Norway. When the great colonizing movement to the West began across the Alleghany Mountains into the valley of the Ohio River and along the shores of the Great Lakes, the conditions of the first settlers were repeated. Among men who find themselves in a wild country, where everyone has like difficulties to face and needs the help of others, there is no room for assumptions of superiority, and each is judged by what he can do. Characters are strengthened, resourcefulness is developed, and there is also induced a sort of recklessness and a disregard of conventions which does not subside for two or three generations. Theodore Roosevelt often said to me that the pictures Dickens drew in *Martin Chuzzlewit* of the West as he saw it contained a good deal of unpleasant truth.

The political change from a government, nominally monarchical and administered by governors sent from England, to republics whose executive heads were elected by the citizens, counted for less than did those influences of the new country which I have already described, because the colonists had long enjoyed self-government for most purposes, and the main lines of their character were already fixed. Nevertheless, the Revolutionary war, and the independence it won, did make a difference. To have (no doubt with the aid of France) thrown off the sovereignty of an old and powerful state after defeating its army, heightened the self-confidence of the people. To have done this in the name of Liberty, though there had in fact been very little that could be called oppression, quickened their march towards the goal of absolute political equality, and gave them a faith in abstract principles and high-sounding phrases which had theretofore been absent from the normal American as from the British mind. Faith in liberty would have been altogether wholesome and inspiriting had it not made the republicans of the four generations that followed the Revolution forget that there are other powers beside those of kings which may threaten liberty.

One cannot speak of the great separation and all the consequences that followed it, not merely for England and America but for the rest of the world, without asking what would have happened had the political link with Britain remained unbroken. Though the colonies must, as time went on, have become with their growing population even more fully self-governing than they had been before 1776, they might have continued to be united to the mother country so far as foreign relations were concerned, for the connection would have been for the benefit of both, since France and Spain still held territories to the south of them, and the navy of Britain would have served the colonists then as it serves Australia and New Zealand to-day. The misfortune was, not so much that independence came, as that it came in the way it did. None of the current assumptions by which enthusiastic optimists beguile themselves has less basis than that of believing the thing which has in fact happened to have happened for the best in the long run. In 1776 things might have happened otherwise, and happened far better. England suffered from the fact that the English Government was then in weak or unskilful hands. There were strong and wise statesmen in England, but they were not in power. The men who controlled affairs were some of them short-sighted and incompetent, some of them narrow-minded, some of them subservient to a perverse and obstinate king. As there are moments in history when the presence of a great man turns the current of events and saves the situation, so, also, are there times when his absence means disaster. Independence, virtual or legal, ought to have come gradually and peacefully as the natural result of American growth. Coming as the result of a war it left bitter memories behind, which poisoned the relations of the peoples for generations thereafter. Supposing that, controversies having been amicably settled and difficulties adjusted, independence had not come in 1776—1783 let us indulge ourselves in a little post-prophetic speculation as to what the course of events might have been. Would there have been a Revolution in France? A collapse of the Bourbon monarchy would probably have come, but there might have been no volcanic cataclysm had there not been in America a successful proclamation of democratic doctrines which when they spread to Europe brought republicanism into the realm of actuality.

Would the economic development of a still colonial America have advanced so swiftly as it did under an independent republic? Would the adventurers who streamed forth into the western wilderness, and built up new states there, have been as bold and pushful as were the American frontiersmen from 1790 to 1850? And if development had been slower might it not have moved upon better lines? Has not the American West grown too fast?

Let us take another point. Might not the struggle over slavery from 1820 onwards have been less hot and angry, and been guided to a less terrible *dénouement* than that of civil war? Might not the influence of the mother country, and the example which she set in 1834 of abolishing slavery in the West Indies and South Africa, have brought about a peaceful compromise? If the American people had not consisted of states claiming sovereignty though united in a federation, but had continued to be divided into a number of practically self-governing colonies held together by some looser tie, each of these would probably have solved the problem for itself, on the lines it thought best, with the co-operation and advice of the mother country. The British government would not have attempted to interfere with slavery in a masterful way, but the public opinion of an undivided and impartial British people might have been a potent factor, suggesting gradual emancipation and the best method of attaining it.

So far the balance of advantage would seem to incline in favour of a continued connection between Britain and the colonial Americans, just as we in England to-day think the connection of the Self-Governing Dominions with Britain and with one another to be for their interest quite as much as for ours. But there is an objection fit to be considered. It may be said, and it was at one time natural to say, that the American Revolution saved liberty for England as well as for America, and at least hastened its victory in Continental Europe. As Sir George Trevelyan has admirably shown in his history of the American Revolution, the revolutionary war came near to being a sort of civil war in England as well as America, and the English Whigs of that day held the freedom of England to be involved in the struggle. A crushing defeat of the revolting colonies would, doubtless, have been a set-back to Whig prospects, but if those concessions to the colonists which Chatham and Burke desired had been made, no such result would have followed. The forces which were already at work, both in Britain and in continental Europe, were, as we can now see, far too strong to have been overborne by a succession of kings like George III, or even by a succession of kings like Frederick II of Prussia. It is to-day plain enough that the extinction by economic causes of the relics of feudalism, and the disappearance of the old reverence on which hereditary monarchy had relied, would, sooner or later, have overthrown absolute government in France, Germany and Italy.

On the other hand one consideration rises to the minds when we regard the consequences, not merely to the British stock, but to the world at large, which the continued political union of Britain with America might have involved.

Might not a highly civilized state embracing both the United Kingdom and the American people, a state already possessing the most powerful navy in the world, and spreading out, as it was evidently destined to spread, over the territories Britain has subsequently appropriated in the south temperate zone, a state dominating the sea, possessed of resources in money as well as in men far beyond those of any other state in the world,—might not such a state have become a menace to its neighbours? Would not the sense of preponderating power have tempted it to abuse that power, to seek a world dominance, to create an antagonism to itself, such as the Empire of Charles V created in the sixteenth and that of Napoleon created in the early nineteenth century? These, however, are speculations, seductive but unsubstantial, and the higher we carry the airy edifice, piling hypothesis on hypothesis, the more unsteady become the upper storeys. I will not try to build the edifice higher, content to have suggested a topic in which imagination may revel at leisure.

Returning from this digression, let me note another influence, which, beginning about 1830, has ever since determined the channel in which the energies of the American people have tended to flow. This is the development, without precedent in the annals of mankind, of wealth derived from what Nature had bestowed on a new and amazingly productive country. During the nineteenth century immense fertile tracts have been brought under cultivation, forests hewn down, coal and iron, silver and copper, worked on a vast scale, while the transport of these products to the Atlantic coast has provided employment for hundreds of thousands and, latterly, for millions of workers. Nearly all the more vigorous minds in the nation were drawn to a business life and politics suffered, partly by the greater attraction business exerted, partly by the habit, which preoccupation with commercial interests fostered, of leaving politics to be managed by politicians. The large-minded thinkers who adorned the last years of the eighteenth century left few successors. Most of the brilliant literary group that gave lustre to the middle of the nineteenth, were born before 1830. That development of the universities which has rendered inestimable services to America since 1880 had scarcely begun. These causes made the material progress of America run ahead of its progress in letters and arts, though there was no diminution in the total volume of intellectual force which the nation possessed.

Now let us turn to another phenomenon of supreme consequence in its ultimate influence on the population of the United States. Immigration from Europe, which had gone on steadily though slowly from the middle of the seventeenth century, suddenly grew in volume when the middle of the nineteenth was reached. It has not sensibly affected the States with a very large coloured population, viz.

those that lie south of the Potomac and east of the Lower Mississipi, but in the North and West it has reached vast dimensions. This increase was, at first, chiefly due to an outflow from Ireland, where famine was raging. Twenty years later it expanded still further by the arrival of new immigrant swarms from Germany and the Scandinavian countries. Still later, between 1880 and 1890, another flood began to sweep in from Central and Western Europe, and even from Western Asia. While Irishmen had congregated in the larger cities, the Germans, Swedes and Norwegians went to settle on the land. Nearly all of these last, either already knowing or easily learning the English language, soon intermingled with the native American population, and were absorbed into it, acquiring American habits of thought and action. German as well as the Irish immigration had shrunk to small dimensions before 1914, for the German government was trying to retain its subjects, while the population of Ireland had so much diminished, and its economic condition had so much improved, as to reduce the tendency to expatriation. Both the Celtic and the Teutonic stocks were already present in the United States, for both had gone to the making of the British race, so that no great change in the essential racial qualities of American character, as it had existed among the early colonists, followed the influx of these new Celts and Teutons. But the later arrival of such races as Slavs and Italians, Russian and Polish Jews, Greeks and Roumans altered the case. They brought entirely new strains of blood into the stock. They were comparatively uneducated, coming from the lower social strata in their respective countries, and were for the most part untrained in self-government. Very few spoke English, and as they settled in huge blocks, mostly in large industrial centres, they were less readily assimilated. What difference then has their coming made in the character and habits of the American people?

In economic, social, and political life, some results are already visible. Those newcomers, who now form the bulk of the unskilled labourers in the northern half of the United States, have plenty of native intelligence, and a few men of conspicuous talent have already risen from their ranks. But being ignorant and prone to fall under the influence either of foreign propagandists, or of leaders of their own race, they are easily drawn into industrial strife, and are more disposed to violence than are the native Americans. When they acquire votes and are enrolled in a political party, their inexperience throws them into the hands of their chiefs, and makes them an element whose power it is hard to calculate either in elections or when labour troubles arise. But—and this is the point to be noted by foreign observers—they are still unassimilated, and have not yet had time to affect what may be called the normal type of the American people. It remains to be seen how soon, and in what way, they will affect it.

Here we are met by a question which has never arisen before either on so great a scale, or under conditions which enable it to be so carefully observed, a question needing examination by physiologists and anthropologists as well as by historians. There have been many cases of race intermixture, but in extremely few of these have we statistical records sufficient to furnish data for scientific conclusions. The problem may be stated as follows: When two or more races mix their blood what is the comparative importance of blood, i.e. of Heredity, on the one hand, and of Environment on the other, in determining the quality of the race which arises from the mixture? In the United States the child of Italian or Czech parents grows up ignorant but intelligent, untrained to anything but hand labour, yet inheriting certain inborn tendencies and propensities, and possibly, also, drawing from his parents certain beliefs and habits. The boy goes to an American school, where he imbibes the ideas and imitates the ways of the American youth around him, and as he grows up reads the same newspapers, hears the same talk. Unless his parents are well-educated persons, he is eager to forget their race and to become immediately, and for all purposes, an American and nothing but an American. He waves the Stars and Stripes, he sings in the class:

> My country, 'tis of thee
> Sweet land of liberty...

with more effusion than if his ancestors had come over in the 'Mayflower.' Yet the blood remains. He is not, he cannot make himself, altogether an American, divesting himself of the parental tendencies, of the emotional excitability of the Czech, or the impulsiveness of the Italian. To what extent then will these racial qualities pass into and modify the American mass? How far will a crowd, twenty per cent. of which is of Polish or Greek or Jewish parentage, differ from a native American crowd? When three generations have passed, how far will the population of any city, one-half of the blood in whose veins comes from East European sources, feel, think, and act differently from the way in which the people in that city felt, thought and acted thirty years ago, say in 1880, before the East European flood had swollen? The city was then four-fifths English, the rest North European or Irish. In 1960 not more than a half will be of English blood, but all will be English-speaking, and permeated by American influences. Though no one can answer the question I am putting, this much at least may be said. There has never been anywhere an environment of more pervasive and compulsive power than that into which the immigrant is plunged when he lands in America. He seems to melt in it as a lump of sugar melts in a cup of tea. Yet one cannot but believe that the influence of heredity remains. If we discern racial traits in the individual man, and explain points in his character by saying he has a strain of Greek or Polish or Jewish blood, must not the inherited quality of the individuals modify the quality of the mass?

The question can never be fully answered, because causes other than heredity are always modifying national character from one age to another. When, sixty years hence, observers compare the character of the American of 1980 with that of the American of 1880, it will be impossible to determine how much of the change is due to this particular cause. The character of a nation, like that of an individual, is always undergoing changes, too subtle to be discernible at any given moment, but evident after the lapse of years. They are retarded or accelerated in the political sphere by the presence or absence of the institutions and traditions which are continually educating and forming men's habits of thought and action, making the habits flow in certain channels and deepening those channels. But it must be remembered that institutions themselves are always changing, if not in their form yet in the manner of their working. Nothing can arrest either decay or growth except death, and health consists in the power of always eliminating the dying tissues and replacing them by those in which life is vigorous.

Thoughtful men in America are disquieted when they see under their eyes a change passing upon the elements in the population far greater than has ever passed before upon the English stock since it first came to Britain in the fifth century of our era. Some fear a permanent injury to the moral, perhaps also to the intellectual quality of the stock. Others believe that the power of literature and education and the old traditions of the nation will preserve what is best in the essentials of character. Uncertain as the future is, one who has watched the process during many years finds reason for sharing the more hopeful belief.

Having considered the character of the American nation as modified by American conditions we may proceed to its concrete manifestations. Salient features will stand out when we note what the people have produced and how they have faced the crises that have arisen in their career.

The Constitution of the United States, drafted in 1787 and set to work in 1789, may be deemed the greatest single contribution ever made to Government as an applied science. It was less original than some of its foreign admirers have supposed, for the best of its arrangements were not fire-new, but drawn partly from the constitutional laws and usages of England, partly from the Constitutions of the several

States, which were themselves modifications of the laws and usages under which the States had been living when they were colonies. But the structural provisions embodied in the Federal Constitution were so well selected from the materials which lay before the framers, and were so skilfully fitted together to form a compact whole, firm yet elastic, capable of bearing the strain which changing circumstances might impose, that the authors of the Constitution deserve all the praise they have received. The parts of that famous document which experience has most emphatically approved are the sections which create the federal system, and which guard its working by assigning to an impartial and technically competent tribunal the function of expounding what the mind and will of people probably were, and must, anyhow, be taken to have been, when they enacted the fundamental instrument. A federation which was created for thirteen States, covering an area of 335,000 square miles, with a population of about 3,000,000, has been made applicable with far less friction than could have been expected to forty-eight States, covering an area ten times, and a population thirty-six times as large. This system has been taken as a model by every country that has since its date adopted a federal scheme of government, including not only the Republics of Spanish-America, but also Switzerland, Canada and Australia, and also, in a less degree, South Africa and the present Republic of Germany.

Less successful, yet, when we consider the difficulties to be overcome, hardly less skilfully constructed, has been that part of the Constitution which determines the relations of the two chief departments of the National Government—the Legislature and the Executive. No frame of government made to be worked in a large country has ever succeeded, except for short periods, in adjusting these relations so as to combine efficiency, promptitude and safety. The most successful was, probably, the scheme of British Government as it worked for the half century which followed the Reform Act of 1832. Comparing that scheme with the American scheme we may say that the British excelled in a concentration of power which permitted swift and decided action, while the merit of the American consisted in the safeguards it provided against ill-considered action or the usurpation by either department of the proper functions of the other. The one system was built for speed, the other for safety. One provided a method by which decisions can be reached with the minimum of delay, the other a method which averts the risk of decisions not representing the true and deliberately considered will of the majority of the people. The British method is forced to take the risk that decisions may be wrong, the American method the risk that decisions may be dangerously delayed. The capital instance of the latter fault may be found in the controversy which so long harassed America regarding the extension of slavery. The National Government tried for forty years to settle this question, but no settlement could be reached, and the result was civil war. English critics used to think this a fatal blot, and praised the efficiency of their own system, but they have latterly come to perceive that their own frame of government may succeed no better. The British Parliamentary System has for more than eighty years failed to settle a question less formidable, indeed, but always threatening strife and deranging the proper working of its own machinery, that of securing peace and good government in Ireland. Each country has to admit some failures, and neither country is likely to part with its own scheme to adopt that of the other country. Each would prefer to steer its course among the rocks and shoals which it has learnt to know, rather than to venture into what is for it the uncharted sea of the other. Whatever may be the merits of the British system for a nation which inhabits a comparatively small area, few will think that this system would suit a people more than twice as numerous, and occupying a territory more than fifty times as large.

The framers of the American Constitution have been blamed for leaving open the question whether any state had a right to secede from the Union, since this unsettled point ultimately provided an occasion for a civil war in which both sides had what lawyers call an "arguable case." But it must be remembered that if the framers had tried to determine that question in advance, there would have been no Constitution at all. State feeling was so strong in 1787–8 that a denial of state sovereignty would have led to the rejection of the Constitution when it was presented for adoption to the peoples of the States, while on the other hand, to have recognized state sovereignty so far as to permit secession, would have been to open a door to the very evil it was desired to avoid. As prudent statesmen, they thought it better to take the chance that a right neither admitted nor denied would ever be exercised, than to invite the immediate failure of their efforts. Their hope, though falsified by the event, was at the time a reasonable hope, and we cannot blame their choice.

Another criticism made on the structure of the American National Government deserves a passing word because one of its features has from time to time had unfortunate results on diplomatic relations with other countries. The provision made for the conduct of foreign affairs has been charged with inefficiency because, while the function of negotiating with foreign countries is left to the Executive, the confirmation of executive action and the approval of treaties rest with one branch of the legislature, the Federal Senate. The result of this division of powers is, that, though the President can in practice so handle foreign relations as to manoeuvre or precipitate the nation into hostilities, he cannot conclude a binding agreement with any other country. He can bring about war, but he cannot make peace. The benefits of a well-conducted negotiation may be lost because the Senate may refuse to approve, and a deadlock may result, involving the loss of a treaty on which infinite pains have been spent. Foreign nations find this situation embarrassing. They may bargain and compromise, and make one concession after another, and yet discover at last that all their efforts have been wasted. But they are not entitled to complain, because they must be taken to know the provisions of the Federal Constitution, and these provisions may be justified on the ground that an Executive which holds office for a fixed term cannot be entrusted with powers as wide as those which England allows to an Executive holding office from day to day at the pleasure of Parliament. A President may err, by precipitancy, or because he mistakes the mind of the People, so it was thought needful to limit his authority. In England it may happen that an Administration which negotiates with foreign states, can, if it keeps its negotiations secret, bring the nation to a point where it must accept arrangements which it would, if left free, be disposed to condemn. Neither America nor England has yet come near to solving the problem how foreign affairs should be conducted and treaties concluded in conformity with the will of the people. The difficulty lies in the nature of the case, and particularly in the fact that in no country is public opinion sufficiently informed to exert the power which of right belongs to it. The case for popular control of diplomacy is irrefragable in theory, but theory presupposes a fuller knowledge of the facts by the people than any people has yet been able to acquire.

Before I pass from the Federal Constitution let me note three occasions on which its strength and flexibility were tested. One was seen in 1834, when a new set of men, less educated and more reckless than their predecessors, came into the control of affairs with the accession to the Presidency of Andrew Jackson. Had not the respect for the Constitution and the methods of working it been by that time fairly well settled, there would have been a serious dislocation of the machinery. Serious evils did, in fact, follow, but the ship rode out the storm and calmer weather returned after a while. On the other two occasions, under the pressure of civil war in 1861–5, and of a foreign war in 1917–19, some provisions of the Constitution were practically suspended though, perhaps, not legally violated. But on both occasions when the stress had passed and normal conditions returned, the Constitution was seen to have sprung no leaks.

I have mentioned the War of Secession, and as it is one of the great events of American history, two lessons may be noted which a study of its course suggests. One of these is the danger of ignoring or trying to override the permanent tendencies of human nature. As we see the matter to-day, it was not only a crime, but a blunder to bring the negro from Africa and to force him to work as a slave in the midst of a community of freemen. This blunder, committed before there was any independent America, is chargeable rather on England than on the early colonists, though it was the children of the latter that had to suffer for it[1]. Without it there would have been no Civil War, and the Southern States would to-day be free from a problem whose solution is not yet within sight and whose difficulties have been aggravated by the attempt made to deal with the question when the Civil War ended. This was the second blunder. The Federal Constitution was in 1868 and 1870 so amended as to confer the electoral franchise upon the recently liberated negroes. Wholly unfitted to exercise the franchise with ad-

---

[1] The efforts of the Colonial Assemblies of Virginia to stop the Slave Trade were frequently baffled by selfish interests powerful with the British Government.

vantage to themselves, the coloured people fell under the control of white adventurers, many of them disreputable, who, since the white population of the states that had seceded were excluded from the suffrage, enjoyed a free field for robbery and jobbery, and played havoc with administration and finance, holding their power by negro votes. After a few years the southern whites, readmitted to the suffrage, recovered control, and thereafter, partly by force, partly by electoral frauds, and ultimately by a series of adroit legal contrivances, they regained a mastery which they have continued to maintain. The attempt to bestow political power on Africans, ninety-five per cent. of whom were unfitted by capacity and training to use it, had the result which ought to have been foreseen. It exasperated the whites, it injured the negroes, it has perpetuated trouble, and has, indeed, increased the friction between the races. Abstract theory and emotional sympathy for those who had suffered in time past had led the Northern statesmen to disregard the teachings of Nature. But Nature prevailed against theory. It may be true that optimism, taken all round, is better than pessimism, and it is obviously true that sentiment cannot be neglected as a factor in human affairs. Yet optimism and sentiment will always have their dangers. We see many experiments advocated to-day, and some actually tried, not less hazardous than that which the sanguine spirit of Congress attempted in the days of reconstruction after the calm wisdom of Abraham Lincoln had been withdrawn. How easily do men persuade themselves of what they wish to believe!

If the end of the War of Secession was marked by one great error, it was marked also by one act of supreme wisdom. Never was a civil war followed by so little severity towards the vanquished. Though the victorious North had talked of the seceding Southerners as rebels, all sensible men felt how far from ordinary treason their action had been. No one was put to death for any political offence. Trials, to be followed by imprisonment, were talked of, but were put off with the tacit consent of the nation till they silently vanished away. So soon as fighting had ceased, bitter memories began to die out in the North, and presently they died out in the South also. I remember how, when General Sherman, in the course of whose march through Georgia the city of Atlanta had been destroyed by fire, came thither on an official visit less than twenty years afterwards, a leading citizen of Atlanta observed that the people of the city were glad to see the General though he was known to be rather heedless in the use of lucifer matches! It used to be said that the only Southerners who bore memories of the war were the two classes who had not borne arms—the clergy and the women. The reconciliation has now been complete, and the whole American nation is so reunited that from 1912 to 1914 the children of those who fought in the Northern armies and of those who had fought in the Southern armies, with the few veterans who had survived from the war itself, met to celebrate their own or their fathers' deeds of valour fifty years before on battlefields now marked by monuments which all alike honour. This, also, is a lesson to be pondered by statesmen whose vision is keen enough to look beyond the dust and smoke of recent conflicts to days to come, though perhaps still distant, when each people in Europe will be peaceful and prosperous in proportion to the confidence which it can inspire in its neighbours, and the goodwill it can feel towards them.

Time fails me to speak of other aspects of American history which deserve the special attention of the student. Nowhere in the modern world have economic issues exercised so potent an influence on politics. Nowhere has the problem of setting bounds to the power of commercial combinations and of the monopolies which combinations create, given so much trouble to legislators. Nowhere has party organisation been developed to such dangerous perfection. But each of these subjects would furnish materials for a treatise. It is enough to call the attention of Europeans to the wealth of material which American experience furnishes upon these and other questions which perplex, and some of which threaten, the welfare of civilized states. On one topic, however, I must dwell for a moment, because though it was once so familiar as to have become hackneyed, the present generation has begun to forget it. For nearly a century after American independence had been recognized in 1783, at a time when nearly the whole European continent was controlled by arbitrary governments, America stood forth to the world as the sanctuary of freedom. To the oppressed peoples she rose as the bright vision of a land where no man need tremble before king or priest, an Elysium of the West like that described in the Odyssey, where, far beyond the sundering ocean, fresh breezes of liberty were always blowing to refresh the hearts of men. That pre-eminent distinction it has ceased to hold. Freedom has now spread all over Europe. The Marxian Communists have indeed now begun to paint America in the blackest colours, as a land where the power of wealth grinds the poor, and for whose evils there remains no remedy except revolution. If the lines with which fancy decked it out were too bright a century ago, still further from the truth are the denunciations which it now receives. The sober judgment of history will always honour the founders of the Republic, and the people who have brought their Republic safe through many trials, for one supreme example which they gave to the world when it was sadly needed.

America has shown that it is possible to have a government of the people for the people on a scale of unprecedented magnitude, a scale undreamt of by earlier generations. In all the nations of the Old World the habit of obedience to constituted authority came down from the ages when monarchs reigned by force, and by the awe which force inspired. Subjects obeyed because their forefathers had obeyed, and because armies were maintained to compel obedience. When, as in France in 1792, and in Russia in our own day, physical force failed, and authority was no longer defended by the spell of reverence, there succeeded first a short spell of anarchy, and thereafter a force still more brutal and ruthless than that by which the old dynasties had reigned. So too the countries of Spanish America, though they called themselves Republics, showed for many a year after they had won independence, what happens when an obedience based only on fear and tradition has suddenly disappeared. But among the English of America the habit of respecting law and valuing order, though at some moments and in some places shaken, was never broken. When the time-hallowed authority of a monarch died out of the sky like waning moonlight, the authority of the people rose, as the sun rises to rule the day. As the nation swelled in volume, the difficulty of maintaining order in huge populations scattered over vast spaces seemed to grow greater. But the sense that law as the foundation of order is the guardian of common welfare, grew with the nation's growth. A national government whose physical power was represented by an army of less than one in a thousand of the population exercised an authority greater because less contested than authority had ever held in the despotisms of the Old World. The steady march of the national government became so familiar that men wondered at it no more than the rustic wonders at the unchanging procession across the nightly heavens of the constellations which he has seen since childhood. But those who have studied human nature, and have seen what havoc ignorance and passion can work, and how infinitely hard it has been to bring men to comprehend what is really their common good and work together for it, will marvel at America's achievement and deem it one of the longest steps in the march of social progress that mankind has yet taken. If ever those moral forces which have led more than a hundred millions of men, filling a vast continent, to obey that common will which they have provided peaceful means for ascertaining, if ever these forces that have created and preserved the sense of common duty and common interest, should show signs of decay, what hope would remain for the world? Freedom in America, as elsewhere, has been at some moments abused, at others undermined or filched away: but the pride in freedom and the trust in the saving and healing power of freedom have never failed her people, and have enabled them many a time to recover what they seemed to be losing. It is by the moral forces that nations live. *Moribus antiquis stat res Romana virisque.*

Let me in conclusion touch briefly upon some of the causes which make a full and just conception of the problems with which the American people have grappled, and of such solutions as they have found, specially valuable to Englishmen.

What is history but a record of experiments? Each country studies, and, if it is wise, endeavours to profit by the experiments which other countries try. Now the value of experiments varies with the similarity of the conditions under which any given experiment has been tried to those of the country which seeks to profit by the experiment. The more closely the two sets of conditions resemble one another the better entitled are we to draw conclusions and attempt predictions. Hence, Britain can profit better by the experience of America than can any other country, because the institutions and social life of the two nations are based upon old foundations, similar in their origin. Not only the institutions and laws, but also the conceptions of those things which constitute the values of life are just sufficiently different to make us feel their essential likeness. An Englishman can in discussing any question with an American assume as a common starting point certain moral and intellectual axioms which he cannot assume in the case of any other people. The fact that neither people calls the other "foreigners" speaks for itself.

This idea may be put in another way. History has for its subject human nature. It is the record of what man has thought, said and done. It is the lamp by whose light we see human nature in action, and we can understand the causes, the significance, the results of events in proportion to our comprehension of the characters of the men or the nations concerned. When the records of man's doings in the ancient world or the mediaeval world perplex us, this happens because we are so unlike the men of those days that we fail to appreciate their motives, and those mental qualities which are now (rather loosely) called their "psychology." So, likewise, when we try to follow events passing in other countries we are apt to err from want of understanding the minds and impulses of, say, Russians or Arabs or Chinese. This is one of the great difficulties in the conduct of foreign relations. Diplomatists, if keenly observant, come to know the minds of the men among whom they are cast. Statesmen at home know less, and suffer for it, while the mass of the people is often quite at sea, because it misconceives foreign ways of thought. It has been truly said that no people has ever quite understood another. Thus the average man, having no means for judging the feelings and behaviour of foreigners, is the victim of any misstatements or misrepresentations made by politicians or the press, and, consequently, each people wrongs other peoples and is indignant when it is wronged by others. When, as usually happens, one nation takes its impression of its neighbours from their government and their politicians, its judgments are pretty sure to be harsh. Moreover, each people thinks of the other in terms of the majority of that other, not knowing or caring to know how large or small a majority may be, or how many cross-currents may be running through the public opinion of the other. All this is inevitable, but the resulting judgments are so often erroneous and even unjust, that everything possible ought to be done to enable each nation to look behind or through the government of another into the real feeling and wishes of its neighbour nations.

Now, just as the experiments made by America are more profitable to Englishmen than are those made by other countries, so also it is easier for us, if we take a little pains, to understand American minds and feelings than to understand those of any other people. Reciprocal comprehension is, of course, best attained by the largest possible personal intercourse. The more Americans come to England and the more Englishmen go to America, the better for both. But as it is impossible for more than an extremely small percentage of each people to create by this means a genuine mutual comprehension of each by the other, the next best thing is for each to learn as much as it can about the history of the other. Here, again, it is only a small percentage that has the time and capacity for learning from history, but that small percentage ought to include the leading minds, and especially the public teachers speakers and writers of each country. With them it lies to form and guide public opinion in their respective countries. If the Englishmen on whom this function devolves address themselves more largely than heretofore to the study of American history, and acquire from it an insight into the character and tendencies of the American people, they will be far better able to judge current events, and escape from the atmosphere of misrepresentation or exaggeration, or honest misconception, which most of them have been obliged to breathe. The use of a common language does not necessarily conduce to friendship; rather is it often a source of bitterness, because the unfriendly things which are said in one country are carelessly or even maliciously propagated and diffused in the other. Knowledge, however, though it does not always make for goodwill, is yet always better than ignorance, for it may be extended and perfected. It is anyhow, even if less than perfect, the only foundation on which a sound judgment can be based.

Without stopping to dwell upon the advantages, material as well as spiritual, which the friendship of the two nations would secure for both, I will pass to a wider aspect of the situation. In these days, no Englishmen can think of Anglo-American relations merely in their effect upon his own country. Every view will be deceptive as well as defective which does not take in the other great peoples. We must learn to think in world terms. Now the growth of the English-speaking races is the most significant phenomenon of the last hundred years. That growth continues, and is likely to continue. It would be folly as well as presumptuous vanity for members of our stock to undervalue the contributions made to thought and letters, science and art, which the other leading peoples, and especially those of France, Germany and Italy, have made and are making. These contributions have been in some directions as great or greater than our own. But it is the English language that has spread and is spreading most rapidly. It is the English-speaking peoples that have grown and are growing most rapidly in wealth and population, and that now conduct or control most of the commerce of the world. Their influence upon the world at large is, therefore, more potent than that of any other racial stock, and that influence would, if directed to the same ends, make a difference to world progress greater than any other influence could exert. I ask you to think not merely of political influence, though that is a form of action the power of which is most apparent and most calculable, but to consider also another kind of action, that which the opinion, the thought and the example of English-speaking men, wherever they dwell, be it in the United States or in Britain, in Canada or Australia or New Zealand, may exert upon the thoughts and purposes of civilized mankind. I treat that opinion as a single concrete entity, because the possession of a common language, common habits of thought, common fundamental axioms of conduct, together with the fact that whatever is written by the best minds in any part of the English-speaking world affects the best minds of the other parts, does give a kind of unity to the mind of English-speaking men which overrides all diversities among them. Differences of view will, of course, always exist inside each political community, and the views held by the majority in one community may sometimes be opposed to the views held by the majority in another, but just as these diversities do not prevent, but rather tend to develop and improve by intermixture and debate, the progress of opinion in any one country, so will they act in the English-speaking world as a whole, each people contributing to the progress of thought in the other. It may be said that this already happens as between all civilized nations, since they now stand in a "touch" with one another that is closer than ever before. But language counts for much. The common language and the common principles— what I have called the axioms of conduct—bring the different English-speaking peoples nearer to one another than to any other people or stock. Regard them as a community in the widest sense, and suppose its general opinion to be playing round such large questions as those of the maintenance or reduction of armaments, the protection of native races, the freedom or restriction of economic intercourse between states, the extension or narrowing of the functions of government, and the many projects now discussed for the organization of industry by legal or extra legal methods, and further, suppose the experiments tried by each of the several members of the vast English-speaking community to be closely watched and studied by the other members, may we not believe that the intellectual and moral influence of that opinion upon the world at large would be far greater than any one nation has exercised since the dissolution of the Roman Empire? Now the first step towards the formation of such an opinion must be the fuller knowledge, the more perfect comprehension by each English-speaking people of the mind and purposes of the other, not necessarily for the purposes of joint political action, however desirable that may on some occasions be, but in the broadly fraternal spirit which seeks the welfare of all mankind. It is in the development of intellectual and moral sympathy rather than in formal alliances, unions often unstable and sometimes exciting jealousy or suspicion in other nations, that we may find the kind of co-operation which will best promote that welfare.

We see to-day an old world, a world weary of the past, distracted on this side of the Atlantic by a strife which perpetuates itself in creating fresh wrongs that breed fresh resentments and revengeful passions. The time has surely come when a supreme effort should be made to inspire in the most enlightened and far-sighted minds in all the peoples a spirit of goodwill which may replace international hatreds by a sense of common interests and a vision of the blessings concord may bring. The goal may be distant, but it is a splendid goal, one towards which we are bound to strive.

I have spoken of American history as a part of the history of the English-speaking community of peoples. It is the history of that branch which is now the largest, the richest and the least assailable from without, yet whose fortunes are indissolubly linked with those of all the others. Through its three centuries of life in the Western hemisphere it has retained that boldness and resourcefulness and tenacity of purpose which belonged to the ancient stock that came from the Elbe to the Thames and from the Thames to the Hudson and onward to the Mississippi. It has cherished high ideals and holds fast to them still. Will it not be in days to come the glory of the free English-speaking peoples, to whom Providence has given the widest influence, and therewith the greatest responsibility, that any group of peoples has ever received, if they should join in using that influence to guide the feet of all mankind into the way of peace.

THE FOUNDER OF THE FIRST ENGLISH CHAIR OF AMERICAN
HISTORY, LITERATURE AND INSTITUTIONS

SIR W. GEORGE WATSON, BART

APPENDIX

ORIGIN OF THE
SIR GEORGE WATSON CHAIR

IN 1911, when it was preparing its Programme for the Celebration of the Centenary of the Treaty of Ghent (1814–1914) and of the completion of One Hundred Years of Peace among English-speaking Peoples, the British-American Peace Centenary Committee (which had the arrangements in hand for Great Britain) turned its attention to the provision of adequate teaching of American History in British Universities.

It discovered that no British University made definite and adequate provision for such teaching. There was no University in the British Isles which had either a Chair or Lectureship of American History. This very grave deficiency in our educational apparatus the Committee determined to supply; and it placed the Foundation of a Chair of American History amongst the foremost articles of its Programme for the Celebration.

The outbreak of the Great War prevented the carrying out of this Programme more than in part;

and before the War was over the British-American Peace Centenary Committee had been dissolved, handing over its functions to two allied and affiliated organizations which grew out of it—the Sulgrave Institution and the Anglo-American Society.

In 1919 the Anglo-American Society revived the project of a Chair of American History as the first item of its national British programme for the Celebration of the Tercentenary of the 'Mayflower' and the Pilgrim Fathers; and in the last month of that year the generosity and public spirit of Sir W. George Watson, Bart., provided the means to realise this long-cherished plan.

In the date of its foundation the Watson Chair has the honour of being the first Chair of American History established in the British Isles.

The correspondence relating to its foundation, between Sir George Watson, H.R.H. the Duke of Connaught (President of the Anglo-American Society) and H.R.H. the Prince of Wales, is reprinted hereafter, for purposes of record. The warmth of the public reception of Sir George Watson's benefaction, and the appreciation of its international and educational significance, is illustrated by the extracts from leading articles in prominent London journals which are also reprinted.

The foundation fund of the Watson Chair has been invested by the Anglo-American Society, and its proceeds will be used entirely in connection with the purposes of the Chair.

The Chair has been given the broad title of a Chair of "American History, Literature, and Institutions" deliberately; for the reason that it is desired to include all these subjects in the scope of its Lectures, from year to year, and also to draw upon a wide variety of eminent Lecturers, who will be able to interpret American life and history, in its broadest aspects, to the British people.

It is not proposed that the Chair should be attached to any one University, but that it shall be used for the general purpose of stimulating interest in and study of America in all British Universities.

Neither will the Chair be held permanently by one scholar, of a single nationality, but for a period of one or two years by American or British Scholars or public men,—thus drawing upon the best intellectual resources of the two countries, and securing a variety of treatment of the subjects dealt with.

The Committee trust that this Foundation will assist to create in this country a wider knowledge of America to-day, and of the history, literature, and institutions of the great Transatlantic Commonwealth of English-speaking people.

The Chair, it is hoped, will serve as a permanent memorial of America's loyal partnership with Great Britain in the Great War, as well as of the historic ties of kinship which unite the British and American peoples.

Lord Bryce's Inaugural Lecture will be followed, in the Spring of 1922, by a Course of Six Lectures by President Hadley, of Yale University, on "Some American Economic Problems of To-day." These lectures will be given at different British University centres, and subsequently published in uniform style with the present volume.

The Committee of the Anglo-American Society desire to acknowledge the great assistance they received from Sir Francis Trippel in bringing the subject of the First Chair of American History to the attention of Sir George Watson, and in securing his practical interest in the proposal.

All communications relating to the Watson Chair should be addressed to:

THE SECRETARY,

Watson Chair Foundation,

c/o The Anglo-American Society and Sulgrave Institution,

1, Central Buildings,

Westminster,

LONDON, S.W. 1.

THE SIR GEORGE WATSON CHAIR

The offer of Sir George Watson to found and endow a Chair of American History, Literature and Institutions, was conveyed in the following letter to H.R.H. the Duke of Connaught, President of the Anglo-American Society under date of November 27th, 1919:

SULHAMSTEAD HOUSE,
THEALE, BERKS

YOUR ROYAL HIGHNESS,

I have learnt with the deepest interest that the programme drawn up by the committee of the Anglo-American Society in connection with the Pilgrim Fathers tercentenary celebrations next year includes the foundation and endowment of a Chair of American History, Literature, and Institutions of a novel kind in Great Britain.

I agree with the committee that the foundation of such a chair or lectureship would greatly assist in creating in this country a wider knowledge of America, and of its history, literature, and political, educational, and social institutions, thereby knitting more closely together the bonds of comradeship between the two great English-speaking democracies, upon whose good-will and friendship the peace of the world depends.

I also share the committee's belief that, as a permanent memorial of America's loyal partnership with the British Empire during the war as well as of the historic ties which unite our two peoples, nothing could be more fitting than the establishment of such an educational foundation. It would have considerable effect in clearing away the ignorance and the resulting prejudice, which should be frankly recognised on both sides of the Atlantic as the real stumbling block in the way of closer union between the two nations. In spite of the brotherhood of arms during the war, there is still a call for much discriminating labour to banish this prejudice. The diplomatic relations between the two countries would enter upon a smoother path if the far-seeing efforts of the statesmen on both sides were aided instead of hampered by the man-in-the-street; and the commercial relations, which as a consequent natural development must vastly improve, would do so with far more rapid strides if business men were to realise the fact that mutual knowledge means better trade.

Every effort should, therefore, be made to prevent a weakening of the sympathies which have been so greatly stimulated between the two countries by the historic visit of His Royal Highness the Prince of Wales, and it is good politics, good business, good morals, to maintain them firmly on their present high level. To all American residents in this country, or visiting it for business or pleasure, and to all British who have personal or commercial ties with the United States, it is a matter of moment that a reciprocal knowledge and sympathy should grow at a rapid rate and be rooted in a firm soil. And all enlightened men and women who—apart from personal or business interests—are possessed of a wide vision, must also feel an impulse to take advantage of any opportunity of furthering so desirable an aim.

British universities and schools have hitherto given little attention to this important subject. It is necessary to generate a new interest in and make America and its life and thought better and more universally known and understood in this country.

For all these reasons it would be a source of great pleasure and satisfaction to me if your Royal Highness would consent to convey, as President of the Anglo-American Society, my cheque for £20,000 as a gift to His Royal Highness the Prince of Wales for founding and endowing the above-mentioned chair.

The present juncture, when the echoes of the wonderful reception of the Prince of Wales by the American people are still reverberating throughout the world, seems to me a felicitous occasion for expressing the hope that His Royal Highness, on reaching the shores of his native land will graciously accept this free-will gift in the spirit in which it is given for the intended purpose, and allow the Chair to be named "The Prince of Wales's Chair of American History, Literature, and Institutions."

Yours faithfully,

W. GEORGE WATSON.

THE DUKE OF CONNAUGHT'S REPLY

The following is the Duke of Connaught's reply to Sir George Watson, dated December 1st:

DEAR SIR GEORGE WATSON,

Lord Weardale, Chairman of the Executive Committee, has transmitted to me, as President of the Anglo-American Society, your letter of the 28th inst. and the accompanying cheque for £20,000.

I will communicate your letter and gift to His Royal Highness the Prince of Wales immediately upon his arrival and he will doubtless personally address you on the subject; but I cannot refrain from at once giving expression to you on behalf of the Anglo-American Society how deeply we appreciate the high purpose which has inspired your magnificent donation, and the happy choice of the occasion of the return of the Prince of Wales from his most successful journey to give effect to it.

This journey marks, we believe, a momentous epoch in the relations of America and Great Britain. The remarkable and generous manifestation of sentiment which his visit evoked among all classes in America shows how recent events and common ends pursued in fraternal union on the fields of battle have effaced all disturbing memories, and brought the English-speaking peoples into closer touch than at any time in their previous history.

This great achievement you desire to signalise and develop to greater advantage by the foundation of a Chair of American History, Literature, and Institutions, which shall give to the rising generation a new interpretation of the past relations of the two nations, and new hopes and confidence in their future.

It is difficult to imagine a more timely and well-directed benefaction, and the Anglo-American Society, in conveying to you their most cordial expressions of gratitude, can now, as a consequence of your striking and spontaneous intervention, contemplate with greater satisfaction the full realisation of their programme for the due celebration next year in Great Britain and America of the Tercentenary of the sailing of the 'Mayflower' and the Pilgrim Fathers.

Believe me, yours sincerely,

ARTHUR,
President, Anglo-American Society.

THE PRINCE'S LETTER

The following is the text of the Prince of Wales's letter to Sir George Watson, dated St James's Palace, December 4th, 1919:

DEAR SIR GEORGE WATSON,

Nothing could have more touched and gratified me upon reaching again the shores of Great Britain than the announcement just made to me by the Duke of Connaught of your noble gift of £20,000 for the foundation of a Chair of American History, Literature, and Institutions, and this is very pleasing to me as I have no personal connection with the Society.

My all too short visit to the American Continent has convinced me of the common underlying sentiment which resides in all sections of the English-speaking world. Such differences as must naturally exist are more those of form and habit than of substance, and no purpose can be higher than the one to which your beneficence has been directed of endeavouring by educational effort to remove those false impressions which an erroneous interpretation of past history, or of the varying forms of our democratic communities, have created and still unfortunately prevail.

May I, however, venture to suggest that it would be more fitting under these circumstances that the foundation should bear the name of the generous donor, and therefore be known as the Sir George Watson's Chair of American History, Literature, and Institutions?

Yours sincerely,

EDWARD P.

ENGLAND AND AMERICA

From *The Times* leading article, December 5th, 1919.

The foundation and endowment of a Chair for the study of American history, literature, and institutions is an interesting and valuable feature in the programme of the Anglo-American Society for the celebration next year of the sailing of the Pilgrim Fathers three hundred years ago. Sir George Watson has been happily inspired to make the return of the Prince of Wales from his historic visit across the Atlantic the occasion for the munificent gift of £20,000 to this end. By the terms of the programme the donor has the right to have the Chair called after his name. Sir George proposed that it should be known as "The Prince of Wales's Chair," but the Prince, while acknowledging with the gratitude it deserves the gift and the suggestion, thinks it more fitting that the foundation should bear the name of the giver. That is the old tradition and the wisdom of preserving it will be generally recognised. The tenure of the Chair will be in some respects exceptional. It will not be established in any one of our universities, or filled permanently by an individual professor. The scheme proposes that a British and an American scholar or public man should hold the office for periods of a year or two in alternate succession. There may be difficulties in working out the idea in practice, but of its excellence there can be no doubt....

The occupants of the new Chair from both sides of the Atlantic will turn themselves, we trust, thoughtfully and earnestly, to the great task of furthering Anglo-American inter-comprehension. There could hardly be a task nobler or greater. The understanding between Englishmen and Americans certainly can be made much more thorough than it has been hitherto. We have learnt to know each other in war as we never knew each other before. We have now to supplement that knowledge in peace, and the close study of each other's history, literature and institutions is an indispensable part of the process. The neglect of American history in British universities hitherto has been almost complete. From a purely intellectual standpoint that is a serious loss. The interest of observing how a new and isolated society, originally equipped with our own moral and intellectual endowments of three hundred years ago, adapted them, rejected them, and added to them, as the needs of their peculiar civilisation demanded, should fascinate any true student of comparative politics in the wide sense of this last term. A comparison of the results with those which we ourselves have attained, under the stress of European complications, from the same stock of ideas, principles, and habits during the same period would probably yield useful lessons in the practical art of government.. . .

If the professors filling the new Chair are as sharp-sighted and as judicious (as the Prince of Wales, during his American visit) they cannot fail to foster a view saner and more wholesome than at present exists of the actual relations between the masses of the two chief English-speaking democracies, and of the measure of future development which these relations admit. In that way they may do very much to ensure that both will pursue their independent courses in accordance with those "key" ideas which they hold, and have always held, in common.

ANGLO-AMERICAN STUDIES

From *The Observer* leading article, December 7th, 1919.

The vision of the Mayflower Tercentenary Committee and the generosity of Sir George Watson have made possible an educational experiment which must needs have political effect. The new Watson Chair is no ordinary professorship. Its wide range—it covers the history, literature, and institutions of the United States—contrasts with the general tendency towards specialised research. The Chair is unique, too, in being attached to no one British University, and the period of tenure is exceptionally short. It is intended to combine the permanent quality of a professorship with the variety and freshness of annual lectureship, and so to found a school which shall have none of the traditional narrowness of a school. Altogether a most interesting educational departure.

The political interest is, however, transcendent. Though there has been a solid development of Anglo-American friendship since the war, the two peoples have still much to learn of each other. In great things, indeed, Briton and American think alike. But in little things they differ profoundly, and, after all, life is largely made up of trifles. England is compact, homogeneous, socially stable, whereas America is scattered, full of racial incoherence, and socially fluid. It will be for the new Chair to show how these differences of circumstances produce divergencies in detail of temperament and outlook.

The historical method proper to a professorship is specially appropriate in the study of Anglo-American relations. The national life of both peoples is penetrated with a sense of tradition. Both are conscious of the historic past as an element in the present, and an influence in the future. In French history, 1789 marks a breach; new forces emerge and shatter the old State. But in American history, 1776 emphasises a continuity; old forces gather their full strength and complete the fabric of the State. That is why the old uncritical American patriotism represented Independence as the expulsion of certain evil elements from the body politic. That, too, is why text-books can affect Anglo-American relations so profoundly. Anglo-French friendship will not be influenced by controversies about Napoleon, but Anglo-American friendship is impossible without agreement about Washington. The great truth that hope for the future relations of the two peoples must be based upon a sober and just appreciation of the past is in need of special emphasis just now, when a spirit is abroad which treats everything before the war as negligible and talks of a fresh start for a new world. Britons and Americans above all other peoples, have in their bones a sense of the error of such reasoning. There are no fresh starts in human affairs; the consequences of what has been must needs work themselves out for ever and make history by their working. To understand modern America, to interpret, for example, the Senate's recent policy aright, we must know what America has been, and such knowledge cannot come except by that study of American history, literature, and institutions which the Watson Chair has been founded to promote.

INDEX

ABERDEEN, the Marquess of, viii

"AMERICAN," the name misleading, 6

AMERICAN NATION, origins of, 4

AMERICAN HISTORY
President Butler on, viii
Viscount Bryce on
Too little studied in England, 1
When did it begin? 1 *sq.*
First stage, 4
Second stage, 5
Third stage, 7
Value of study of, to Englishmen, 37 *sq.*, 39
Linked with that of other English-speaking communities, 42
(See also Appendix)

ANGLO-AMERICAN FRIENDSHIP
Mr Balfour on, vii
Viscount Bryce on, 40 *sq.*

ANGLO-AMERICAN SOCIETY, v, vii, 46, 49, 50, 51–52

BACON, 7

BALFOUR, Rt Hon. A. J., v–viii

BRYCE, Rt Hon. Viscount, v, vi, viii

BUNYAN, John, 7

BURKE, Edmund, 15

BUTLER, President Nicholas Murray, vii–viii

CHAIR, The Sir George Watson
Prince of Wales on, v, 52–3
Duke of Connaught on, 51–2
Sir George Watson on, 49–51
Viscount Bryce on, 1
Mr Balfour on, v, vii
The Times on, 53
The Observer on, 55
Appendix on origin of, 45 *sq.*

CHATHAM, Earl of, 15

CLIMATE, Influences of, in U.S., 8–9

COLONIZATION, in U.S., beginnings of, 2, 17–22

COMBINATIONS, commercial, in U.S., power of, 33

COMINES, Philip of, 5

CONNAUGHT, H.R.H. the Duke of, Letter from, 51

CONSTITUTION, The American, 23–8
A model for others, 24
Three tests of, 29 *sq.*

COTTON, and slavery, 9

CROMWELL, Oliver, 7

DICKENS, Charles, 10

EBBSFLEET, 7

ECONOMIC ISSUES, their influence on American politics, 33

ENGLISH-SPEAKING Peoples, The, their supreme mission, 43–44

EQUALITY, social, conditions favourable to, in America, 11

ERIC, The Red, 2

EXECUTIVE, relations to Legislature, 25

EXPERIMENTS, American, in government, their value to English students, 37

"FOREIGNERS," English and American not to each other, 38

FOREIGN-AFFAIRS, U.S. machinery for dealing with, 27–8
British ditto, 28

FOUNDATION, The Watson Chair, (see Appendix)

FREEDOM, U.S. not the only sanctuary of, now, 34
American pride and trust in, 35–36

FROISSART, 5

GEORGE III, 15

GERMANIC TRIBES, 5

GOVERNMENT, popular, triumph of, in U.S. 34

HADLEY, President, 48

HAMPDEN, John, 7

HARVEY, 7

HERITAGE, spiritual, etc. of the American people, 6

HISTORY, U.S., 39 (see under American)

HUNDRED YEARS PEACE, 45

IMMIGRATION to U.S., 17–22; Effect on American character, 19

INDEPENDENCE, American, 2, 12, 57

INDIANS, The American, 3, 9

INFLUENCES, upon English settlers in America, 7 sq.

INSTITUTIONS, American, based on like foundations to English, 37
English, in 14th and 15th centuries, 5

INTERCOURSE, between U.S. and England, should be increased, 39

INTERMIXTURE, racial, in U.S., 20–22

IRELAND, outflow from, 18
Problem of, 26

INVENTION, spurs to, 10

JACKSON, President Andrew, 29

JULIUS CAESAR, 5

LANGUAGE, common, does not always conduce to friendship, 40
English spread of, 40–42

LAW, similar origins of American and British, 37

LAW AND ORDER, respect for, in U.S., 35–36

LEGISLATURE, relations to Executive, 25

LIBERTY, 11, 33, 35–36

LINCOLN, Abraham, 31

LITERATURE, influence of European on America, 7

LORD MAYOR, of London, vii

LYNCHING, 9

MANSION HOUSE, London, v

MILTON, John, 7

MONOPOLIES, trouble to legislators, 33

MORAL FORCES, in American politics, 36

MOTHER LAND, 6

NEGRO, problem of, in U.S., 9, 29

NEWTON, Isaac, 7

PARLIAMENTARY SYSTEM, the British, 25

PARTY ORGANISATION, dangerous perfection of, in U.S., 33

PEACE, of world, 43–44

PERRIS, Mr H. S., v

PILGRIM FATHERS, 2, 46, 52

PREHISTORIC, America, 2

PRESIDENT, Limitation to powers of, 28

PROBLEMS, American, and their lessons for the world, 37

RELATIONS, Anglo-American, vii, 40, 50, 51, 54, 56

RESOURCES, of American territory, influence of, 16–17

REVOLUTION, The American, 11–12, 15
ROANOKE, 2
ROOSEVELT, Theodore, 10

SECESSION, War of, 29–31
SENATE, 28, 57
SHAKESPEARE, 7
SHERMAN, General, 32
SLAVERY, 9, 13, 25
SPANISH-AMERICA, 24, 34
SPENSER, 7
SULGRAVE Institution, The, vii

TACITUS, 5
TAYLOR, Jeremy, 7
TREVELYAN, Sir G. O., 15

UNIVERSITIES, in U.S., 17
In Britain, and American history teaching, 45, 50, 54, 56

WAKEFIELD, Sir Charles, vii
WALES, H.R.H. the Prince of, v, 52–53
WAR, The Civil, in U.S., 29–31; Clemency after, 32
Of Independence, 12
Of 1914–1918, 47, 49
WATSON, Sir W. George, Bart., v, vii, viii, 1, 46, 49–57
WEALTH, in U.S., 16
WEARDALE, Lord, 51
WEST, The American, 10, 13

Printed in the United States
By Bookmasters

Printed in the United States
By Bookmasters